Wakefield Press

the lactic acid
in the calves
of your despair

Ali Whitelock is a Scottish poet and writer living on the south
coast of Sydney with her French chain-smoking husband. This is
her second poetry collection. Her debut collection *and my heart
crumples like a coke can* was published in 2018 by Wakefield Press; a
UK edition will be published by Polygon in 2020. Her memoir *Poking
seaweed with a stick and running away from the smell* was launched
to critical acclaim in Australia (2008) and the UK (2009) and she
has read at festivals and events in Edinburgh, Ireland and Australia.
Her poetry has appeared in *The Moth, American Journal of Poetry,
Glasgow Review of Books, Bareknuckle Poet, Pittsburgh Quarterly,
Tahoma Literary Review* and all sorts of other rather fabulous places.
You can read more about Ali right here: www.aliwhitelock.com.

praise for ali whitelock's
and my heart crumples like a coke can

'This is brilliant. Funny, heartbreaking and a bit wonky. Now my
internal monologue sounds like an Ali Whitelock poem (except
not as good).' Graeme Macrae Burnet, author of *His Bloody Project*
(shortlisted for the 2016 Man Booker Prize), *The Disappearance
of Adèle Bedeau, The Accident on the A35*.

'Whitelock's gifts to poetry are many. These include showing
how poetry doesn't have to be written for a minority in
order to be first-rate.'
Saturday Paper

'Ali Whitelock writes a poetry of excoriating tenderness.
Whitelock is Bukowski with a Glaswegian accent and a nicer
wardrobe.' Mark Tredinnick, poet and author of *The Blue Plateau,
The Little Red Writing Book, Blue Wren Cantos,
The Lyre Bird & Other Poems*

'In these times when antipodean poetry is dominated
by stay-in-line competition poets I find this collection
by Ali Whitelock honest, invigorating and refreshing.
I'm putting this book right on my top
shelf of favourite poetry published in Australia.'
Dr Brentley Frazer, *Bareknuckle Poets Journal of Letters*

'I didn't even want to review Whitelock, I just wanted
to turn back to the first page and start reading again.'
Simon Sweetman, *Off The Tracks NZ*

'Whitelock is very funny. Her titles alone will have you in stitches often enough. With that said, every poem in this book is a deadly serious poem, just with huge portions of witty observation and black humour so expertly added it is never at odds with her subjects.'
Edward O'Dwyer, *Glasgow Review of Books*

'This book is heart-wrenching and, in ways I can't quite explicate, entirely affirming. The poetry manages to be both pithy and almost hysterically funny, not an easy mix to achieve. Whitelock captures this duality perfectly, taking a stand-up comedian's incision to pretension and human foibles.'
Magdalena Ball, *Compulsive Reader*

'She's a social satirist who holds up our world and makes us burst into laughter.'
Rochelle Shapiro, author of *Miriam the Medium*

'One of the wittiest, liveliest and most moving collections I've read in recent years. These poems evoke the best of Bukowski and Ginsberg while being the unique product of a contemporary female mind, a mind that is hilarious, provocative and – remarkable.' Kevin MacNeil, author of *The Brilliant & Forever, The Stornoway Way*

'Ali Whitelock's observations are funny and playful, there is a real honesty to her work and it is in no way pretentious, it's the kind of poetry that I want to re-read even before I have finished reading it.'
Edward Crossan, poetry editor, Polygon, Edinburgh

praise for ali whitelock's
poking seaweed with a stick and running away
from the smell

'Remarkably life affirming.' *Sydney Morning Herald*

'A hilarious, no-misery memoir.' *Scotsman*

'Candid and rhythmic ... humour is her safeguard against the terrible things she tells us.' *Sunday Herald*, Glasgow

'Charmingly cynical.' *Scottish Review of Books*

'Joyous!' Julie, Waterstones, Lancaster

'Every once in a while you come across a story that will stay with you long after the final page. This is one of those stories.'
Chronicle

'... a funny, shocking, bittersweet account of growing up in probably the most dysfunctional family in Scotland in the 70s.'
Greenock *Telegraph*

'... her book isn't a whinge-fest. Far from it. It's a funny account of growing up in a Scottish family of battlers.' *Advocate*

'Pure nostalgia with funny bits – Ali Whitelock must be Billy Connolly's comedy love child.' Laura Marney, author of *Nobody Loves a Ginger Baby*, and *No Wonder I Take a Drink*

'A raucous romp through a dysfunctional Scottish family. Whitelock's storytelling is a wee delight.'
Mandy Sayer,
author of *Dreamtime Alice* and *The Poet's Wife*

'do not speak to me of pain'
has been nominated for the 2020 Pushcart Prize.

'the dandruff in the dry scalp of your longing'
has been nominated for Best of the Net Anthology 2019.

the lactic acid
in the calves
of your despair

ali whitelock

**Wakefield
Press**

Wakefield Press
16 Rose Street
Mile End
South Australia 5031
www.wakefieldpress.com.au

First published 2020
Reprinted 2023

Cover designed by Liz Nicholson, Wakefield Press
Edited by Julia Beaven, Wakefield Press
Typeset by Michael Deves, Wakefield Press
Printed in Australia by Pegasus Media & Logistics

ISBN 978 1 74305 704 9

NATIONAL
LIBRARY
OF AUSTRALIA

A catalogue record for this
book is available from the
National Library of Australia

CORIOLE
McLAREN VALE

Wakefield Press thanks
Coriole Vineyards for
continued support

To all our mistakes, regrets and broken hearts and the words we can't quite find.

And for Thomas, always.

contents

author's note

When people ask me what my poems are about, I want to say, '*oh, you know, grief, despair, hilarity, goats, cancer, custard, the solitary hair on my father's smallpox scar corkscrewing from his upper arm like a mung bean on a sheet of damp paper,*' that kind of stuff. But you can't say *that* – not in the author's note at the front of your own book. So let me say this instead: some five years ago, my father died unexpectedly. I was with him when he died. We had a shitty relationship. He was a shitty kind of guy. But grief is grief and it sneaks up on you in the most unexpected of places, like today at the cafe when the waitress told me the cake of the day was Black Forest gateau and I thought *he'd have ordered that* and wept into my decaf soy latte. An hour after he died, I stepped out of the hospital into the abnormally bright Scottish sunshine and made the decision that from that moment on I would live my life differently; that I would take my life by the balls. And so I took, what's generally regarded as the insane decision, to give up my day job in order to pursue my dream of writing full-time.

the lactic acid in the calves of your despair is my third book. When I'm not writing, I can be found reading my work at rather fabulous places such as the Edinburgh Fringe, Edinburgh International Book Festival, La Mama Poetica in Melbourne, the Brett Whiteley Gallery in Sydney and at many other events throughout Australia, the UK and Ireland. I can also be found (too frequently) dreamily googling chateaux for sale in French medieval villages with little patisseries on the corner, where hair-netted ladies know my name and sometimes slip a little *tarte au pommes* or *millefeuille* into my bag, practically unnoticed.

And so, dear reader, although your google searches may differ greatly from mine, it is my sincerest hope that as you climb the mountain of your life, you too will come across occasional hair-netted ladies thrusting little *profiteroles* and freshly made *creme brûlées* in your general direction and it is my dearest wish that as you climb, the lactic acid in the calves of your own despair will not burn too deep.

ali whitelock, 2020

in the silence of the custard

night crept in, stumbled and fell at my feet
badgers keeked from hedgerows
window wipers wiped, grouse tails flashed, patsy
cline played on the stereo i listened in the dark and fell to pieces.
while you drove like a fuckwit, up single
lane roads that cut into the mountain
like the waistband on a pair of too-tight pants.
the ugly woman behind the bar knew your name
took our coats, showed us to our table
and as you sat sleeveless, the solitary hair
in your small-pox scar corkscrewed from your upper
arm like a mung bean on a sheet of damp paper—
something of you finally stretching toward the light.
you ordered the fish and chips i ordered the same.
i wanted you to see i was like you. and when
the food came, we lifted our forks in unison
cracked through the batter of our steaming
haddocks lined up our chips on our buttered
breads added our too much salt and in between
gulps of our respective white teas you asked me what
kind of car i was driving now. i asked you about
your greenhouse tomatoes.
the thing is i didn't know what it was i couldn't quite say.
and later when we would order
the apple pie with the hot crust and frozen
middle, in the silence of the custard
the closest i could come to it was
i don't hate you anymore.

i am the sea

that january
prestwick beach

the sea heaves. swallows herself down
like cough syrup in thick slow gulps. we'd sat on this rock
just two days before, both of us with our backs to the world
staring out across and into
the thickness.

i counted a thousand and one seagulls that day
watched them huddle together, balance like storks
on a single orange leg the other nestled up in the warmth
of their soft white bellies as they, with uncharacteristic
patience, waited for the rain that would surely fall

and when the wind whipped up, andrew
jumped from our rock pulled his emerald green kite
from his rucksack tore off down the desolate beach his kite ploughing
a trench in the sand behind him, eager for the gust that would
lift it to where it wanted to be

and every few seconds he'd turn around
and run backwards untangling cords and calling out across
the increasing distance between us, 'c'mon on, ali! c'mon!' and i heeded
his call, jumped from our rock and ran as fast as i could
in jeans frozen stiff as though they'd
been pegged on the line

in an overnight frost and i shrieked
with the gladness of finally being here with him—
and no black clouds could ever threaten this day for us. he kept on
running and turning, turning and untangling till finally a gust obliged
and his emerald green kite soared skywards and free—as free as
we are ourselves if only we'll listen.

we'd parked the car just up there by mancini's
snack van, closed for the winter now, its magnum ice-cream posters,
faded and neglected, flap listlessly in the wind and the menu promising
hot chips and curry sauce hangs on the outside wall,
saturated by rains gone by forcing

words to fade, corners to curl and brown
moisture spots to appear in the most unappetising of ways.
we'd laid our picnic out on this rock, poured tea from our tartan thermos
ate buttered rolls, dunked mcvitties chocolate digestives and talked and
talked till the sun slipped off her shoes, turned out the light
and slithered into the black dreams
of the irish sea

and days later with him already
too long gone i am sitting on our rock with my back to the world.
the sea heaves still. i watch her swallow the sadness rising
in her throat, as broken-hearted waves throw themselves
at the feet of a shore that really couldn't
care one way or the other.

not much of a mother in four parts:
part I

i had my baby dead before she was even born
cot death leukaemia fatal blood disorders affecting
one in a million newborns. then there'd be the choking
on the coin, i'm frantic, turn her upside down, slap her back
her face turns blue she stops breathing. then the
anaphylactic shock a single peanut, her windpipe
swells i race to emergency her face turns blue
she stops breathing. repeat repeat
re-fucking-peat.

i marvel at women falling pregnant at the drop
of a fedora risking their hearts on the first rung
of the telescopic ladder of eternal pain. when i turned
thirty-nine the gynae said, *if you're going to try for a baby
you'd better hurry up. relax,* i told him, *i'm fertile*—
i'd been pregnant twice before. he carried on tapping
his notes into his computer muttering how he wished
he'd had a dollar for every woman over forty who'd
ever said that.

we gave it a go. if i'm honest, half-heartedly.
our fedora never dropped, it barely even tipped
then came the shadow on the ovary.

the day before the hysterectomy i drove my friend
to the airport, she was off to the bahamas to cook for
the much too rich and famous. as we hugged goodbye
she whispered *i'm sorry you'll never be a mother.*
i cried all the way home. i never thought i'd have made
much of a mother. for the same reasons for years i resisted
having a dog. it is how they worm their way in till your
heart is mostly holes like a swiss fucking cheese then
before you know it they have you in a rickety cage
wearing a hard hat and carrying a lamp, your rickety
cage swinging precariously as you are lowered down
the mine shaft of your soul. once in your mine the beam
from your lamp will fall upon your heart slumped
on top of a coal wagon. you will remember you threw
it there many suns and moons and saturns ago, it was not
in the best of shape, but you will remember it was still beating.
you see the scabs. you remember how they got there.
these scabs have served you well but they are dry now,
it is time to pick them off. as you pick you understand
that to love is not to tiptoe around the crust of your soul, rather
it is to descend into the fire of your molten core without a harness,
asbestos suit, or dry ice; it is to suffer third-degree burns;
it is to gasp for breath; it is to watch many canaries die.

now is the modem of our discontent

when the internet went down that morning,
and wouldn't come up for another twenty-four hours, neither
of us knew what to say. i spent half the day on the phone to telstra.
the *positive-customer-relationship-specialist's* script
said how sorry he was. he couldn't say how long
the service would be down. at the end of the call he asked
if there was anything else he could help me with today. i told him i couldn't
think of anything. when you came home from
work that night the red light on the modem was still blinking.
i set the table. poured the wine. though neither
of us would speak through dinner. after dinner,
with a good five hours ahead of us and no gateway through
which to connect to the rest of inhumanity,
you, who normally comes to bed at two in the morning,
came to bed at nine that night where i lay
reading a book that had once been a tree. i rose frequently
in those long dark hours, walked past the modem, its red light still blinking,
and when finally dawn came and the red light had turned green
i tore open my laptop checked my emails updated
my status searched for suggestions
on things we could say over dinner should
the internet go
down
again.

the great fucking wall of china

it's no biggie.
it's what they say when something's not big, they
shorten phrases boil them down reduce them like
cream in a pan on a low blue flame. it was christmas.
the radiographer put the condom on the wand, inserted
it, asked if i was doing anything special this year—
like i'm at the fucking hairdresser having my
roots done. then he found something behind the remaining ovary
and things went from being no particular biggie
to being a great big biggie. they removed it a week later.
for four long days i couldn't sit upright. i lay on my back,
imagined the worst, counted the skylights on the lounge
room ceiling (there were four), read, *The Stornoway Way*
by Kevin MacNeil then ached in a different way this time
at the beauty of language and turns of phrase and for
the wind ravaged islands i'd turned my back
on too long ago.
on day five i could stand.
day six shuffle, day seven asked myself how hard
it could be to just stumble up to the organic store
to get the miso and the tempe and the other fermented
shit the naturopath told me to get. well really fucking
hard is how hard that turned out to be. after thirty metres
i admitted defeat, lowered myself to the kerb at the entrance
to the bp station as the price of unleaded dropped and
drivers hysterical at the prospect of cheaper fuel screeched

in on two wheels mounting the kerb where i sat flopped
forward like a geranium in need of a drink.
        then a mercedes pulled in and parked
at the pump. the well coiffured driver glanced across
at me, her eyes smarting momentarily with benign concern
before turning to the pump and selecting, not the cheap ethanol
fuel, but the super duper expensive fuel, the one that cleans
your engine and blah di fucking blah and makes you feel
guilty in the same way watching a volvo ad is designed
to make you believe that one day all of your children
will die and it will be entirely your fault.
        then the well coiffed woman hung
the hose back on the pump without even shaking it to get
the last of the drops and by the look of the alligator handbag
would not be fishing out the supermarket docket for the two
cent per litre discount before continuing on her road paved
in twenty-four carat gold.
        not like the month before in chinatown,
when pain smashed and i crumpled just outside the lucky world
supermarket where they sell the bitter melon and the chicken
feet in the five kilo bags. the chinese man came and sat quietly
beside me on the kerb, only he didn't speak english and i didn't
speak chinese, but he looked at me. and his look asked if i was
okay and was there anything he could do. and my look said to
his look, thank you, there's nothing you can do, but i can't tell
you what it means that you stopped to ask. then his look said
to my look, have you seen a doctor? and my look said to his look
i have, but so far they say there's nothing to see.

then the chinese man rose
from the kerb, went into the supermarket where they
sell the bitter melon and the chicken feet in the five kilo
bags and came out with a carton of chrysanthemum tea,
poked a straw in the hole handed it to me and i drank
it down and his look said to my look, i wish there was
more i could do. and my look said to his look you've
done enough already. thank you for this tea. it is delicious.
how thoughtful you are, how caring. and as i swallowed
the last of the tea his look said to my look, take care
of yourself won't you. and my look said to his look,
i promise you i will.

then back outside
the bp station where the chrysanthemum tea of human
kindness was in short supply i clambered to my feet and
started back on the road that may as well have been the length
of the great fucking wall of china toward the organic store,
its neon sign blinking like a mirage in the unimaginable
distance. i got my miso and my tempe and fermented
tofu and stopped a hundred times on the way back
home as the price of unleaded dropped some more.

a week later i saw the surgeon,
a man who wouldn't know chrysanthemum tea if it sat
centre stage with a thousand watt bulb shining directly
on it. he asked how i was going. i told him i'd been
drinking chrysanthemum tea, eating fermented tofu and
avoiding deep-fried food, the naturopath said it keeps cancer
at bay don't you know. then he sighed his condescending

sigh as though i'd just told him i'd met three witches in the
woods who'd casually suggested i boil the liver of a blaspheming
jew, throw in a couple of turks' noses and strain it all through
wool of bat, whatever the fuck that is. he took my blood
pressure, listened to my chest, shone a light in my eye
and told me, *if you're predisposed to cancer, no amount
of chrysanthemum tea's going save you.*

scottish dirt

when my father's best friend tired of smashing
the hammer into my father's head, he threw it
to the side, grabbed his *here's one i prepared earlier*
baseball bat & laid into my father's body like
he was trying to put out flames in a fire he
wished he hadn't started.

(dragging my father's body across the scottish dirt
and into to the car wasn't my favourite; his broken
false teeth clacking in his mouth; his knee caps hanging
like a confused sack of jigsaw pieces; the blood
the car upholstery wouldn't absorb.)

when the judge concluded my father's best friend
wasn't guilty of grievous bodily harm, my father held his
head in his hands like a coconut he never wanted to win,
three circular indents from the hammer blows overlapping
on his crown like a venn diagram intersecting where
friendship, lies & dog-eat-dog collided.

a week after the court case my father's best friend
sent two of his people around with another message.
that night when we came home we found my father's
broken body splayed on the carpet, limbs at obtuse
angles like a wooden marionette dropped out
of the sky.

the police said there was nothing they could do. when
they left the house our normally placid dog cleo ran
them out of the driveway, the best of her small
barks sparking at their ankles.

i took to answering the door that summer with a
bread knife behind my back. my uncle paid two men
with neck tattoos in an idling ford cortina to guard
the house like we were living in a scottish episode
of the sopranos.

my father was frail for a long time after that.
weeks lumbered by, summer leapfrogged autumn
and requiemed into the winter that went on forever.

both my father and his best friend are dead now. both
their pasts buried deep in the scottish dirt. though a hundred
seasons on, snowflakes from that winter still fall,
land on my lashes,
obscure my vision
fuck up my hair.

when the flurries are at their thickest
i turn away from idling parked cars
cross the street when i see a tattooed man
flick the off button when re-runs of
the sopranos come on.

a poem walked into a bar

thrust a sheet of A4 paper into my hands, said,
'here, have this.'
'what do you mean?' i said, 'what is it?'
'it's a poem,' the poem said. 'a poem?' i quizzed.
'aye, a poem,' the scottish poem replied.
'well how come you're just handing it to me?' i said.
'because,' the poem said, 'i've been watching you from the driver's
seat of my big poetry bus and every time i pull up at your stop
i see you hunched over your laptop, only stopping now and again
to get a cup of that kombucha or whatever the fuck it is you're drinking
these days, or to rub the RSI in your forearms from your too much typing
and i see you agonise trying to find exactly the right word with exactly
the right weight that conveys the exact emotion you are trying
to get down on the exact page exactly no one gives a flying fuck about.'
'sorry ... your big *poetry* bus?'
'aye, that's right. for the last eighteen months—you bashin' away
at the keys like a maniac lookin' aw tortured—i know hemingway
said, *writing is easy all you've got to do is sit at the typewriter*
and bleed, but you didn't have to take that quite so literally.
so here. put your pen down, take the day off and have this poem. it's free.'
'a poem for free?' i said. 'i can't just have a poem for free!'
'of course you can. you've earned it—sure there's an imprint
of your nose on the screen of your mac to prove it. so here, before
i change my mind. take the fucking poem.'
'well, i' won't lie, it is tempting,' i said, 'but what about the bleeding?
what about the struggle? what about the endless fumbling at three am trying

to find the notepad and pen on the bedside table to get lines and ideas
down before they disappear forever?'

'a poem doesn't *always* have to be *that*,' the poem said, sternly, 'the poem
does not always demand you sink ankle deep in clay from the weight
of the oxygen tanks on your back as you climb mount kilimanjaro
every time you lift your pen. sometimes a poem will simply land
on your lap, as though it were merely exhaled from the lungs
of, i don't know, fucking angels or something, in one single breath.'

'but what kind of poem can come from not bleeding, not fumbling,
not struggling?' i implored.

'this kind!' the poem snarled, shaking the piece of A4 paper under
my nostrils, like it were a crisp cotton bed sheet flapping in a violent
glasgow wind.

i took the sheet of A4 paper from the poem's hands and surveyed it.
i mean it looked like a poem, had the same weight as a poem, christ
it even smelt like a poem. i held it up against the window as a surgeon
might an x-ray of a poet's breast and pink hues of sun filtered through,
illuminating rosy cheeked cherubs, succulent vines and a heart
still full of poems to come.

'look,' the poem said, 'i haven't got all day. if you don't want this poem
there are plenty of other poets who do. and by the way those oxygen
tanks look heavy.'

'well, now you come to mention it, they are pulling down on my
scoliosis quite a bit. okay poem you have convinced me. i will accept
your effortless gift.'

i took the piece of A4 paper from the poem's hands, clutched
it to my heaving breast, its perfect pearlescent beads
of clichéd morning dew melting like a child's tears against
my undeserving but forever grateful heart.

'oh poem you are a marvel. this is truly a wondrous gift!'
'a marvel?' the poem shot back, 'i am not a marvel. do not hold me
in such high esteem. do not prostrate yourself before me at the alter
you have created filled with the incense and mooncakes of your own
imagining. do not inflate me with the bellows of your longing,
nor throw unnecessary logs onto the embers of my existence simply
because you are in need of warmth. next time you pick up your pen
and find yourself ankle deep in the clay of your own making, lay
down your oxygen tanks, summon to mind the exhalations
of angels and remember, i am not a marvel.
i am merely words
and rhythm,
imagination
and truth.'

ode to an eggplant

the eggplants weren't worth ten dollars a kilo
but you'd wanted them so badly, to impress
me with your vegetarian lasagne, the one you
make with the béchamel, the fresh italian tomatoes
the parmigiano reggiano—the one you make when
you sense the urge to run is back in me again

i'd stood in the corner by the dishwasher, watched
you peel the garlic slice the onions grate the cheese
salt the eggplants to remove the bitterness that always
comes at the end of things

then you fried them in cold pressed extra virgin olive oil—
the expensive one we bought that day at the blue mountains
tea room when we stopped in for home-made scones with
blackberry jam and clotted cream and drank them
down with two pots of french earl grey (*the fancy one*
they sell in david jones with the wild blue
flowers in it, do you remember?)

i gasped when i saw you crush four giant cloves
of russian garlic into the tomatoes *to boost your immune*
system you said, the virus in my chest still crackling
ten days on each time i breathed in and out and laughed—
which, granted, wasn't very often back then

too salty, you said, grimacing after the first mouthful,
and me i could barely tell—my tongue and tastebuds
long since dead, everything now tasted of air

well, did you rinse them before you cooked them? i asked,
you know, to remove the salt?

of course i did, you replied, casting me a sideways
glance, as if i'd just asked if you'd ever really
loved me.

how;

how he runs through the facts of his boy's
death like he's ticking off stages in a home
renovation gone wrong; how the gyprock came
late—how gyprock is always late; how the idiot
in the hardware store sold him the wrong
fucking screws; how at one stage he had to take
down all the walls and start again; how the electricians
were called but still the lights wouldn't come on;
how the entire school turned out for his funeral; how
they replaced all the plastic with copper and still
the plumbing wouldn't plumb; how he would have
been eleven his next birthday; how the council
granted permission to take down two trees but still
the sun couldn't shine through; how when the terrible
rains came his gutters collapsed; how he braced himself
for when his roof would finally be gone; how he watches
cartoons with his youngest—superman rescuing every
other man and his fucking dog; how they scattered
his ashes in the skateboard park; how humpty
fucking dumpty, how bob the fucking builder;
how he keeps his room exactly as it was; how
he knows he clings too tightly; how he tries
to be strong; how he ropes a tarpaulin
tight around his heart.

kmart sells out of cheap fans made in china

what my friend said in an email:
it feels like a thousand years since i last saw you.
what i replied: *make that two.* then i told her i'd been writing.
in between sweating. so much sweat i could've filled lake eyre.
too many days in australia at forty degrees, the world's heating
up. then trump got elected. then i went to the shopping mall,
which is depressing but the turbo-charged air con is awesome.
then i got to thinking about the word awesome, how it's over-used,
how only yesterday i asked the waitress for a second jug of milk
for my pot of earl grey & when she brought it i said *thanks that's awesome.*
then mum's friend's dog died & i wrote an email of condolence.
then my father died & i read the eulogy. then we sold the house
on the four lane highway two years after the attempted suicide.
then we moved by the sea.
it was winter.
the sand was cold. frozen air stencilled salty snowflakes onto
my cheeks, the wind slurped my hair north like god was sucking
up the final strands in a bowl of holy spaghetti. then temperatures
fell further till the zygotes of my grief froze. then trump got elected.
now the heat blisters. people can't afford to turn on their air con.
kmart sells out of cheap fans made in china. single mothers
fill coke bottles with water, freeze them to stick between their breasts
trying to find comfort in nights as scalding as the days. guilt prevents
me from turning on our air con. some nights i lie awake for hours crisping
at the edges like a fucking meat lover's pizza. someone said count sheep.
i tried, but they turned into air conditioners. i must have counted a thousand

one night. watched them frolic in brittle meadows, skip gaily hand-in-hand
across the cracked beds of evaporated creeks & finally, when sleep came,
my dreams were filled with people searching for water in a world dying
of thirst. now the ice caps are melting & the fucking polar bears are dying.
then trump got elected. i tried to write a poem about this heat but it ended
up being about the daughter i never had & sadness crept up behind me,
put its hand over my mouth and pulled me backwards into a filthy dark
alley i hadn't been game enough to venture into before. then the mechanic
said i needed a new car because my gearbox was about to fall out. and the
mounts were fucked. i don't even know what mounts are. my sister
is in edinburgh. i worry she thinks i'm wasting my time writing poetry
when i could be earning money in a real job. she sent me photos of the
writers' museum & told my niece *i'd* be in there one day & even though
it will never happen it still made me feel proud. then i rearranged
the lounge room to make the place feel more spacious (i had two dining
tables and ten chairs in there). then my friend told me she'd rearranged
her lounge room too & i was meant to drop in to see how awesome
it looked only the summer arrived, mum's friend's dog died.
trump got elected. now all the fucking
polar bears are dead.

scotland, winter, 2014

nobody knew what was wrong.

we sat around your bed every night in the vinyl chairs for four
hours that felt like four hundred in our far-from-expert white coats,
hypothesising, googling, guessing – lying, mostly, to ourselves and
to you.

i feared your thin; your evaporating legs; the blanket engulfing
you; the mattress you were disappearing into. the thing was you
seemed a little better that night. you even bobbed your head in time
to the jingle of the Cadbury's chocolate ad blaring from the telly
in the corner of the shared ward.

your cousin tommy came that night. the chocolate eclair your
sort-of-wife brought the day before sat on your bedside cabinet
uneaten, its brown paper bag saturated in the grease it had leeched.
the tube of condensed milk i'd brought to try to tempt you into
eating something sat unsqueezed.

when the bell rang at eight o'clock mum swung her handbag over
her shoulder, leaned in, kissed you on the forehead said we were
all off to the pub did you want to come. nobody laughed. i rose slowly,
tried my best to look disappointed the four hundred hours were up already
pulled my coat over the layers of my grief felt my way into the solitude

of my gloves tied a scarf around my neck like a hangman's noose
and walked out of the ward past the fat bastard snoring down the
sanitised corridor pushed my way through the heavy swing doors
that keep the fires out and the sadness in.

we stood a while in the car park talking. your cousin tommy told
us you didn't treat your sort-of-wife very well. if tommy was saying
it, it must have been true.

winter fog purred in to the car park weaved itself around our legs
settled on our feet like a fat grey cat as bewildered visitors spilled
from the hospital's infected mouth and into their cars, their yellow
fog lamps casting damp shadows on the empty that filled me.

i stopped off at the pub on my way home with my selfishly flawless
health and perfectly functioning limbs, pulled up a narcissistic armchair
by an indulgent log fire ordered a self-absorbed gin. when the waiter
brought me my gin you were still alive. i raised my glass to the man
you were, the father you weren't and to the health and future
it turned out you didn't have.

steaming pile of shite

i'm not getting another dog again and that's final.
but when i do i'm going to call him *sweetheart*.
i like the idea of calling out *sweetheart* on the street
or at the beach when he ventures, as my old boy hector
did much too frequently, too far away from me.
and hector never came when he was called, unless of course
i had a sausage in my pocket. but on the days i stood
sausage-less, i'd watch him bound away from me
to the far end of the beach completely ignoring
my cries, his canine GPS leading him directly
to the red pin dropped in the centre of a circle
of japanese tourists eating fish and chips on the sand.
and the japanese gasped and laughed and awwwwwwhhed
with the joy of his invasion and that sense of privilege
when a dog who does not know you, makes his way
directly *to you*, his tail wagging as though you were
the most important person on this fucked-up planet,
and if you can matter to *this dog, this lowly* fucking
dog, perhaps you're not the steaming
pile of shite you believe
yourself to be.

not much of a mother in four parts:
part II

after the hysterectomy my seventy-year-old friend Hamish
asked if it would affect my ability to have children. under
normal circumstances i'd have laughed, taken out my highlighter
drawn a fluorescent yellow circle around his stupidity. this time
i merely nodded, thanked him for asking and the waiter brought
the scones, the danish, the strong black coffee. i ended up getting
two cats. there were six kittens in the cage to choose from.
i chose the two that sat alone in opposite corners to each other—
each of them staring out into their own very separate horizons.
i have always gravitated in the direction of lovelessness.
this relationship i'm in now has love on demand. it is a two litre
carton of full cream milk that sits in the fridge. there is no best
before date, the level never goes down and i have yet to pour
my cornflakes into my morning bowl only to open the fridge
door and suffer the crushing disappointment of no milk.
sometimes i don't know what to do with love like this.

so there's the woman with the white hair & the daughter called pumpkin

& she's got the shop that sells the lamps & the tables
& the vases & she paints everything in gold leaf except
for the replica louis XV side tables which she paints
a creamy colour & she calls that french wash.
i sit at the cafe next to her shop with my dog. i take him
everywhere with me. she asks if i'm from europe. i tell her
i'm from scotland, how i've been here for twenty years,
how i miss europe dreadfully.
then the woman with the white hair & the daughter called
pumpkin tells me gold leaf is very popular in europe, that
she comes from portugal & used to paint nails in a beauty
salon. my sort-of-sister-in-law is a nail surgeon—it's what
they call it these days. it used to be a manicurist.
i went to a house once in greenacre where they have
the drive-by shootings. i knocked loudly on the door.
when it opened, the shimmer from the gold velvet couch
the gold plated lamps the gold painted walls blasted out
like an over-tinselled christmas tree that's lost its fucking
mind.
so the woman with the shop & the white hair & the daughter
called pumpkin had a chandelier & she was selling it for eight
hundred & eighty-five dollars & that's australian dollars
& that's not cheap. the crystal teardrops looked like glass but
the woman with the white hair told me they were crystal,
that she painted it with gold leaf herself—too much gold leaf

in my opinion—and that shot the price right up. then she told
me the crystal came from czechoslovakia & i have always
wanted to go there—to prague—if you must know it got
flooded recently too much rain, it's happening all over
the world now.
i knew a man from prague once we waited tables together
in sydney. he was tall and thin wore milk bottle glasses
& grey polyester pants full of static electricity. he reminded
me of a test tube wearing a big red nose. he used to clasp
his hands behind his back, call women 'madame' & men 'sir'
like proper waiters with manners might do, say, in melbourne
or just outside the dandenongs where you can get a devonshire
tea and breakfast all day if you've a mind—no wait he wasn't
czechoslovakian but hungarian, that's right i remember
now, so this woman with the shop & the white hair
& the daughter called pumpkin didn't have enough customers
so she had to close down. she said her gold leaf may not
be popular here but it sure as hell'd be popular in europe
& that her gold leaf lamps & tables & vases & replica
louis XV side tables would sell for double at least, if she
set up in the likes of budapest or lisbon or krakow, well
the europeans are more refined don't you know. the last
day of her shop was sunday. i was passing by with my dog.
i always walk my dog on sundays & every other day for
that matter. she was loading up her car with the last of her
lamps & tables & vases & she offered me the chandelier
for two hundred dollars & that's australian dollars & that's
certainly cheap. then she reminded me the teardrops
weren't glass but czechoslovakian crystal, and she banged

on again about the gold leaf & how it's very european
& yada yada yada and i gazed at that chandelier, imagined
it hanging above my dinner table & how the light would refract
through the czechoslovakian teardrops casting european
shadows on my macaroni cheese. i took the dog home
and got the cash. i can put up with too much gold
for a price like that.

if life is unbearable

1. take one glazed pudding bowl from the high cupboard where you keep the shit you never use.
2. wipe off dust.
3. open drawer.
4. take out non-slip mat so bowl does not slip.
5. cast your eye upon the folded floral apron that reminds you of the victoria sponges and warm kitchens of your youth.
6. close drawer.
7. enter walk-in pantry, lean back against wall, exhale. excavate self for motivation to move on to step 8. (consider heavy plant and earth moving equipment.)
8. pull self together. gather required ingredients from pantry shelves. arrange on kitchen bench.
9. open packet of chia seeds you bought when optimism was still a thing.
10. take each seed and survey to ensure quality and organic-ness. (each seed will be unique. this will only add to the pudding's wonder.)
11. smile if you have it in you (though this step may be substituted with dried egg).
12. add one third chia seeds to two thirds coconut milk (or coconut cream it makes no difference. to anyone.)
13. reject all stainless-steel utensils. as if stains were something any of us could avoid.
14. mix with a wooden spoon. it just feels kinder.
15. if deserved, add chocolate powder and/or half a cup of freckled banana (mashed).

16. mix again. as well as can be expected.
17. wonder why you are even bothering.
18. allow to stand.
19 in the warmth of the right kitchen the seeds will expand to their fullest potential.
20. taste.
21. if life is unbearable, a little sugar is permitted before serving.

the word cunt

my friend bronwyn and i discussed
the word cunt on tuesday after it had rained
non stop for seven weeks and my succulents
were juicier than they'd ever been.
i described the colour of the sea that day
as eucalyptus, a sort of smoked mint, an opaque sage.
she asks me what sort of a cunt thinks like that?
she reckons i spend too much time alone. then she says
since you're so po-fucking-etic how else
would you describe the sea?
a woman's heart i said. a cauldron
of cold fish tears, a crone in love with the moon, the sloshing
fluid of god's inner ear.

for a while the darkness was all we could stand

in those first few days without him,
there were times i'd find thomas in the pantry,
lights off sobbing against the wall. for a while the darkness
was all we could stand. at night we ladled more than spooned
his cold knees nestled into the soft backs of mine, the sadness
in his bones whispering to the sadness in mine. when we
hugged, i burrowed into him as though i were trying to wear
him, as though i were trying to dress myself in the three piece
suit of him. and once i was safely in behind the small shirt
buttons of him, when all of me was inside the dark of the
smallest russian doll of him, i could assess the damage
to our hearts—the weakening of our walls, the blocks
in our valves, the reluctance in our millimetres
of mercury.
eventually we moved the contents
of our two hearts into one, it just made life simpler.
still it was hard to find a place to put our two of everything—
the cordless kettles of our loss, the six slice toasters
of our woe, the breville juicers from under the sinks
of our misery. we spent months decluttering—stream-
fucking-lining, buying space-saving storage thingies
from ikea, pushing the sideboard of our grief from
one end of our sardined
hearts to the
other.

natural born goat killer

After James Tate's 'It Happens Like This'

i keep my kitchen scraps for my neighbour's
goat in a bag on my kitchen bench. sometimes i worry
the goat will die because i've unknowingly put something
in the bag that's poisonous to her. sometimes i'm so paranoid
i check on the internet to make sure things like coriander
stems, star anise, used earl grey tea leaves are not toxic
to goats. i read once parsley was poisonous to parrots. who knew?
& my fears of goat toxicity are not founded on nothing. my friend
carolyn's goat milly died after her neighbour unwittingly
fed her seemingly innocent rhododendron leaves. rhodo-fucking-
dendron leaves.
& even though i am vigilant i still worry something deadly
will slip into the bag unchecked, the goat will eat it, her belly
will swell & she'll fucking die, most likely in excruciating pain.
the vet will be called. questions will be asked, '& what *exactly*
did you feed this goat?' the vet will demand of its owner.
'i didn't feed her anything!' he'll reply, 'my neighbour
brings all her food!' then the police will be called in. a burly
sergeant will come to my door flash his ID, 'okay so exactly
what *did* you feed this goat?'
'only scraps from my kitchen,' i'll plead, trembling, 'you know,
celery leaves, parsley stalks, star anise, the odd rotten tomato.'
'well the fucking goat's dead,' he'll say, slapping his truncheon
into the palm of his left hand, 'and i need answers. i'm sorry,
but ah'm gonna to have to take you in.' then he'll handcuff

me, throw a blanket over my head & lead me through
the mob of mourners & protestors already gathered outside
my front door screaming, 'why did you kill her?! what did
that poor goat ever do to you?!' a dozen police officers will form
a human shield around me, manhandle me into the back
of the paddy wagon, turn on the siren & screech through
the streets to the station for further investigation & possible
strip searching. once there they'll make me hand over my shoelaces
& belt, read me my rights & i'll get to make my one solitary call.
i'll call my lawyer alissa, who'll tell me she's never
had to defend on a goat trial before—she normally
only does conveyancing, divorce, that sort of thing,
but she knows some hot shot lawyer in the city
who specialises in goats & never lost a case yet.
i'll heave a sigh of relief, lie back on my wafer thin mattress
in my surprisingly spacious cell. hours will pass. from my bed
i'll be able to see the flat screen TV at the night sergeant's desk.
i'll be all over the nine o'clock news with that fucking
blanket over my head journalists jostling, shoving microphones
& iphones into my face. someone in the crowd will throw an egg,
yell out, 'MURDERER!' the pushy journalist in the front row
will thrust her microphone near down my throat, 'the death
of this goat has rocked this community,' she'll scream, 'people
are calling you a murderer. do you have *anything* to say?!'
'yes,' i'll cry, whipping the blanket off my head, 'i have this to say.
i have faith in the legal system of this land. i believe my innocence
will be proven. the internet police need only sequester my laptop
& look at my browsing history to know i am vigilant about every
scrap i put into that goat's bag.' the reporters will scribble

frantically before another barrage of microphones is thrust
into my face. 'but do you have anything *else* to say?' another journalist
will roar above the frenzy. 'yes,' i'll say, my voice cracking
tears spilling, 'i have this to say: no one loves goats more
than i do in this little town.'

in
the
event
of
a
lack
of
oxygen

HOLD the earth in your hands / be careful—she is hot / talk
to her tenderly the way you might your mother at the end of
her days / honour her / place her somewhere she might rest/
perhaps the mantelpiece between your bone-china swallow
mid-flight & your fake brass barometer the shape of a ship's

wheel that will not steer us out of the storm we are in /
despite her dishevelment, tell her how lovely she looks /
offer her tea / a scone / horlicks if it still exists / slip her
feet into soft slippers / massage her shoulders rounded
from the burden you have placed on them / cradle her
in your arms /

now go to the mountains / yes, go / facetime will not suffice /
tell them you are sorry / return with no selfies—this is not the
time / now go to the rivers / listen to them / let them tell you
their stories / do not interrupt with your lies about your
recycling / like you are not guilty of slipping glass jars

& clean cardboard into the wrong bin / now get down on
your knees & beg their forgiveness / do not worry their
banks are no longer muddy your levis will stay dry /
understand in the event of a lack of oxygen no yellow
masks will drop from the sky / remove your stilettos /
leave all your personal belongings behind / tiptoe

past earth's bed / leave a note under her pillow / apologise
profusely / tell her you'd drunk too much / that you weren't
in your right mind / that you didn't realise just how much
you'd loved her till she was gone /

speak when she speaks to you / if your shame will allow
it make eye contact / answer her questions with an honesty
that will feel alien to you:

> *yes we had ample opportunity / yes money*
> *was more important than water & air / yes*
> *we're tired of our empty promises too / yes coal*
> *yes carbon emissions yes methane yes plastic /*
> *yes dollars yes pounds yes euros yes yen / yes*
> *vegan yes sweatshops yes you warned us no*
> *we didn't listen / yes we saw the signs yes we*
> *ignored them / yes we heard the bees are in*
> *default & the banks are foreclosing all hives /*
> *yes we should have planted more lavender*
> *more rosemary more bottlebrush / yes flooding*
> *yes fire yes species extinction / yes we should*

*have been kinder / yes we should have stopped
to think before we fucked her / yes we should
have pulled out sooner / yes oral contraceptives
yes STDs / yes we should have used a condom /
yes we are sorry / yes
look at this mess now.*

scene from trainspotting as it relates to self

so what happens is tommy's
a health freak pumpin' iron, liftin' weights, an aw that shite.
then lizzy breaks up wi' him 'cause he lost the porno video
of him and her shaggin'. then his heart's that broke he loses the plot
and gets on the smack only he shares durty needles, gets HIV
and dies. then mark, who's really ewan mcgregor, asks one
of the mourners how tommy died, wiz it pneumonia
or cancer? cause usually that's what you die of if you catch the HIV.
turns oot it was toxoplasmosis from the kitten tommy'd bought for lizzy
when he was tryin' to win her back. right wee cute thing
it wis tae only she was done wi' him and told him to stick his kitten
up his arse, so he was left wi' it and what wi him aff his face a hunner
per cent of the time the poor wee cat was neglected, shitin' and pissin'
all over the floor where tommy lay aff his face and that's how he caught
the toxoplasmosis. we had a house full of cats when i was growin'
up. my da' always used to say they were filthy fucken animals that wan
day we'd aw get a disease aff them and die a horrible death just
like what tommy did. only i've had cats aw ma life noo, and that's aboot
fifty year and ah'm no deid yet, but my da' is and it wisnae cat shite
that killed him either, i'll tell you that for nothin'.

the primary reason you may find yourself fucking a psychopath*

is because you had your ovaries removed & a complete
hysterectomy & you are now frisbeeing towards the surgically
induced menopause the surgeon did not think to tell you about.
[of course there are other reasons why you may consider
fucking a psychopath however this reason is a very
good one]

another very good reason might be that you are in a long term
relationship and you are feeling, well you can't quite put your finger
on exactly *what* you are feeling, but bored seems to be the closest
you can come to it

this is because the one thing your body was meant to produce
& spent the last ten years trying to produce has amounted to sweet
fuck all & you are now spending a lot of your time wondering
what the fucking point of everything is

and although you will not yet have had the conversation directly
with your body, your body will know there ain't no baby ever
coming from this here womb

and your body will not know what to do with this knowledge
[but your mind will find something to do with it]

and one day as you apply your make up you will become
acutely aware that the day will come when your breath will
no longer make the little steam circles on the mirror
in front of you

& you will feel like your body has failed to do the one thing it
was probably meant to do, which is the one thing that made
it different from a man's body [apart from the five thousand
other things]

and your body will now feel like a kelpie without a flock
or a mitsubishi mirage you could not get rid of for free in the
trading post for spares (*even if you wanted to*)

and it will now go in search of new things it can do with
itself however it will not really know where to start

but it will take a stab in the dark & start by showing itself
off to anyone who cares to look at it and it will attract the
attention of many men as though it were sending
up a flare from a lifeboat lost at sea

and the lifeboat will be full of the too many other women
who couldn't quite put their finger on it either

and one of the men who will see the flare will be the caring
considerate man who's loved you for more than twenty
years & knows a woman in trouble when he sees one

however what he does not understand (*and no one understands
really*) is a woman in trouble prefers the attention of a psychopath
in spectacles held together

with scotch tape who somehow knows if he listens to her & nods
his head in the right places, he will find his way into the driving
seat of her body that's currently listed on the trading
post for free

with its relatively high mileage

complete service history

and one (lady) owner.

[* *excerpt form larger work as yet untitled*]

the lactic acid in the calves of your despair

let me pour tea into the holes of your grief, add drops
to your eyes now emptied of tears, wrap your wounds
in gauze soaked overnight in my deepest concern.
let me wring out the sleeves of your thick woollen
jumper now drenched in the song of your mourning.
let me peg it to dry in what little sun there is, utter
sounds that comfort, make tea that soothes.
let me know all i can say is
i'm so sorry
here drink this tea
then the sorry thing again.
let me wave you off from the base of the Grampians
of your anguish, fill your backpack with squares of dark
chocolate and emergency dried fruit—nourishment,
you will need it along the way. know as you climb your calves
will burn with the lactic acid of your despair. breathe
into your pain—know it will recede.
sit down a while and drink from the tartan thermos
of your healing. and when you reach your cairn,
lean in to the wind, look down into your valley
of loss. marvel at the distance you have covered.
at how far you have come.

O cloud

O cloud—sometimes you are long & pointy with a dorsal
fin & look like a rubber pike hanging on the wall of a log
cabin in the canadian rockies with a sign under it saying
the one that got away.

Once you looked like a man with black hair exactly
like my husband with no eyes, banging out chords on a fender
american deluxe & dreaming of a tama drum kit with gold plated
hardware that can never be.

But mostly cloud, you look like a great white tumour
growing exponentially on god's own brain, pressing down
on his cerebral cortex, impairing his vision leaving him unable
to dive headfirst into the mediterranean to save the tiny unripe
fruit hanging from the barely established sapling of Alan Kurdi's
life.

Then there was the other time god, so out of it on tumour
medication, was unable to prevent the air strike on Omran
Danqueesh's house, leaving Omran shocked & bewildered,
his wee boy fingers dipping into the blood seeping
from his too little head—

O fluffy unsweetened mouthfuls of fairy floss! O lumpy
cushions of puffed up whiteness—no amount
of chemo can shrink you.

O enormous grey & sometimes charcoal swollen
hearts stuffed full of aunties over forty, weeping for the children
they left it too late to have.

O fat silver bladder inside a cask of cheap chardonnay
from liquorland.

O ample misshapen knobbly thing like the black carcinoma
that grew on the dog's elbow & the vet couldn't cut off
for fear the cancer would spread.

O mildly irritating husband with the sedentary
job who does not exercise & promises to give up smoking
& pays monthly membership to the gym but never fucking
goes.

O smoke ravaged lungs of a husband who will probably
die young & float up to heaven on a soft warm cloud like an ikea
feather doona straight out of the dryer.

O great bulging jaws of clouds that huff & puff & blow
the unaffordable house down.

O three little pigs in a homeless shelter.

O too young dead husband strumming gently on a harp
that was never his instrument.

O glorious skinny cigarettes he sometimes rolls by hand
using pouch tobacco with less chemicals though he still
has a packet of ready rolled in his man-bag at all times.

O abundant, probably empty promises of a life lived long
together.

O second hand smoke rings from god's own fag.

not much of a mother in four parts:
part III

it is always the middle of the night. after emergency
triage she'd be admitted to intensive care. there'd be tubes,
and drips, the machine that beeps the sonar requiem of the grief
stricken whale mourning the loss of her calf. and i'd spend
the last of those nights curled up beside her—i'd be sobbing,
she'd be the one stroking *my* hair telling *me* not to cry.
my daughter would have had a strength i could never know.
i'd keep her hand in mine, read her a bedtime story
tell her i loved her three hundred million times

> hours would
> crawl days buckle
> her clutch fade
> fingers cool—
> she'd drift like
> snow and the
> night would
> take her.

the woman in the wide-brimmed hat at the funeral
home would ask about the eulogy, the order of service,
the psalms, the prayers, the power point slides. too sweet
smelling candles would flicker, casting shadows of dead
children dancing discreetly in corners. i'd have to choose
her coffin; i'd have chosen pink with diamanté handles
images of Elsa and Anna around the outside; Olaf
on the lid. and i'd insist on the softest fleece
to line it.

> grief would fill me like concrete.

NOTES from the six week course entitled: 'a beginner's guide to writing poetry'

course tutor: god in black turtleneck
voice: booming
ego: 1 x large
promises: the moon

GOD welcomes us to the course by pointing out where
the kitchen is, how the toilets are just along the hall then
bangs on about things called villanelles and haikus,
pantoums and sonnets and dazzles us with tales of
past students who went on to become published
poets themselves.

AND the frisson of hope we paid so heavily for *(and
which made up the bulk of the course fee)* breezes in
through the door left deliberately ajar, sprinkling each
of us liberally with fragments of hope that land like
dust from the wings of moths, as we settle down
with our pens and our hopes and god's
promise of the moon.

slide one

A SONNET HAS 14 LINES
I JOT down this potentially important piece
of information. no one else in the room does.
i try not to let this fact bother me. writing a sonnet
sounds hard. the fourteen line thing disturbs me.

this is only slide one. i remind myself i have come
on this course to learn what i do not know. i take
a deep breath, lay down my pen and try to relax
into god's anointed hands as my fingers clench
tightly around his promise of the moon.

slide two

IAMBIC PENTAMETER

GOD moves swiftly through this description
as if it were so obvious there were no need to even
mention it. just like when he decided to create light
and suddenly there just *was* light. i scribble frantically.
no one else does. i tell myself i am no less poet than
anyone else in this room except maybe for god down
the front in his turtle neck sweater. i breathe deeply
into the brown paper bag i keep on hand for occasions
such as this, wipe the sweat from my brow as the ink dries
in my pen and the moon (*as outlined in the course
terms and conditions*) sits smirking down the front
with its arm around god as we move terrifyingly
onto slide three.

slide three

FORM

APPARENTLY the poem escapes from the form.
why does the poem need to escape? what is it escaping
from? where should it be running to? i scribble frantically.
no one else does. i cup my hands over my ears,

try to hum an upbeat tune as hope fades in my
pen and i try not to swallow my song.

slide four

a b a b b

a a b b

a a b b c c d d

a b a b c d c d

don't.

even.

fucking.

ask.

slide five

COFFEE BREAK

GOD tells us to be back in the room in twenty
minutes. i spend nineteen pacing, drinking instant
coffee dunking biscuits from the arnott's selection
included in course fee fantasise about shoving
a custard cream or a buttery scotch finger
right up god's arse along with his promise
of the moon.

    the

      night

        drags

          on

slides don't stop. rules trample me under
their hooves and the tiny wooden bird trapped
inside the cuckoo clock of my calamity
bursts out through its chalet doors, its normally
unfettered cries of cuckoo! cuckoo! now a stifled
fuck you! fuck you! as the final slide of the night
is projected onto the screen i never
want to look at again.

final slide

HOMEWORK: WRITE A SONNET
ON seeing this slide my mouth forms an O
my hands clasp the side of my face like
the live model for edvard munch's *The Scream*.
i reach for my brown paper
bag. the moon is obscured.
the moths are all dead.

    WHEN i get home i look at my notes:
a sonnet has fourteen lines

             iambic penta what? WTF look this up
a poem escapes from the form??? (no fucking idea)

    does god exist? what's with the goatee?

ALL week words won't birth. i sit in a warm bath
with a notepad and pen trying to soothe them into
existence. i am in the thickest part of the forest.
i have a piece of bread in my hand. my father
is a woodcutter, my mother a psychopath.

I VENTURE deeper into the forest trailing breadcrumbs
behind me. i find a spot by a trickling brook, set up camp,
light a fire, wait quietly for words to appear. if i know
anything it is that i must be patient. night falls. from the safety
of the darkness an A appears. stands alone in the clearing.
minutes pass. some Rs shuffle cautiously into view, followed
by some Bs and some Os, some Xs and some Ys, then entire
alphabets start creeping out from behind moss covered
rocks offering themselves up to me like sacrificial
          lambs.

I SPEAK in a soft low voice. tell the letters how lovely
they look today, the way their Cs curl inwards at the top
and the bottom, how elegantly their Ss bend like the neck
of the most magnificent swan. i praise the peaks of their capital
Ms, compliment the space inside their Os, remark upon
the tails of their Qs, which are poetry themselves. then
i enchant them with a tune on my magic pipe, till hundreds
more letters are pouring onto the page, forming words
and dancing gaily as though they had not a single care
          in the world.

AND once i had enough letters to make my sonnet
i threw down my pipe, rounded the letters up, twisted
their arms up their backs, held a gun at their heads
told them to lay the fuck down in their fourteen
          lines and no one gets hurt!

THEN suddenly the Rs burst free followed by the Xs and Ts
the Ps and the Vs all of them screaming, *we won't
be part of your sonnet and you can't fucking make us!*

    i ended up in a straitjacket

    then they took me to the asylum.

WHEN i got inside i saw god in his black turtleneck
and another three poets with goatees. *hey you guys*, i said,
fancy seeing you here. how you been? but none of them
answered on account of the medication and the leg-irons
    digging in to the weeping sores of their sonnets.

THEY locked us up in the same padded cell. i was
the only one without a goatee. i asked the guard
to loosen our straitjackets a little, maybe open
a window, let in some air. time ticked by. the sun
flossed her teeth, pulled on her pyjamas and
    made way for the dark.

HEY, *that reminds me*, i said to the poets,
whatever happened to that promise of the moon?
the poets gathered up their leg-irons, shuffled
to the window, pointed out through the bars
at the bald white orb hanging aloof in the
midnight sky, *there it is*, they said,
    we told you we'd deliver.

Extracting the Stone of Madness
Hieronymus Bosch
Courtesy Jheronimus Bosch Art Center, The Netherlands

do not speak to me of pain

A response to 'Extracting the Stone of Madness'
by Hieronymus Bosch

after my father died, i saw him everywhere.
driving the bus. in the hardware store discussing the unique
benefits of one lawn mower over another. waving at me from
    from coffin shaped clouds.

    when i was trying to fall pregnant, all i saw were
pregnant women. some with one already in the pram. a second
toddling alongside the wheels. a third selfishly baking
    in wombs fertilised with blood & bone.

    now everywhere i look i see exhausted women.
this one in a yellowing field. a white knight-less horse in the
distance. fat red book on her head. red is her colour.
        knowledge becomes her.

    she looks on at the man banging on about
his pain. she listens. wilting like a garden of artichokes
planted too close to the frost. the drum of her heart, heavy
as a load of un-spun bath towels hauled from the washing
        machine & hung on the line
           never to dry.

    the surgeon with the funnel on his head
(that no one seems concerned about) makes his first incision.
I see this all the time, he says, hacking into the man's head
foraging for the stone of madness, *particularly in men your age.*

A very serious condition—far more painful than that of the inferior
woman-stone. I mean the average man-stone could easily render
a man unable to take out the bins, cook a meal—even feed the
oxen! Indeed, the best he could perhaps manage might be to
lift a tankard of ale to his very lips!

the woman slumps forward
on to the table that might topple
if she leans too hard.
she is not used to leaning.

it is not that she has no sympathy for the man.
just she's had her own lonely years of period pain, then the ovarian
cancer, the ovariectomy, the appendectomy, the hysterectomy & now
the diverticulitis that has appeared out of nowhere & there is talk
of a man with a funnel on his head removing
the diseased part of her colon.

but she will cross that moss covered bridge when
she comes to it. for now there are bins to take out, oxen to feed,
rabbits to stew—with or without artichokes, it will depend
on the crop.

& she knows her own stone of madness
is growing now too. taking up space in her head like her
dead mother's sideboard she did not want that now sits in her garage
gathering dust & guilt. but she will not have it removed.
she will learn to live with it.

it is what exhausted women do.

it is different to forgetting

there are some things you can never un-know.
it is different to forgetting. the nature of forgetting
is such that one day an image you would prefer
never to see again will possibly re-appear
when you least expect it, like say the image
of your father disembarking from a jumbo jet
in sydney and showing up on your doorstep
unannounced on an otherwise
ordinary sunday morning.

you will answer the door. against your better
judgement you will invite him in to the gentle
green paddocks of the life you have spent the last
fifteen years weeding and mowing, reaping and sowing
and although it will not be his *fullest* intention,
he will somehow manage to crush the trumpets
of your daffodils, ring the necks of your lemon
scented geraniums, drain the tears
from your weeping bluebells.

but the image i would prefer to un-know would
be that of thomas and i with hector on the vet's
cold floor. thomas is cradling hector's head, i am
massaging his mane, both of us are wailing at our
own invisible walls. the vet administers the injection.
i hold hector's gaze, place the tip of my nose against
his, whisper for him not to be scared, caress

his soft velvet ears, softly sing him a dog lullaby –
as though he were merely leaving us for sleep.

once he was gone, thomas pulled a kilometre
of paper towel from the dispenser at the vet's sink
scrunched it into a ball, sunk his wet face into it.
the vet stood back, said he was sorry, handed us
another kilometre of towel before respectfully leaving
the room and us alone with our newly dead boy.
i lay down the length of him, told him i had loved
him like no other human had ever loved a dog –
which even i know is too big a call.

when the vet came back, although i knew it was daft,
i asked if he was sure that hector was dead. the vet
bent down, gently pulled back hector's eyelid, shone
a light deep in to what was no longer a sparkling
eye famous for prising sausages from the melting
hearts of unknown admirers, but the dull opaque
eye of a whole dead fish displayed
on the fishmonger's slab too long.

eventually thomas and i got to our feet, took each
other's hand, readied ourselves to leave. as we walked
away from hector, out of the surgery and towards the car,
i did what i could to turn the internal siren of my grief
down to the correct therapeutic dose.
a few drops in an oil burner is fine.
too much ingested will kill you.

the treeless hill

(i remember the day they took nanny away on the stretcher;
grampa running after the ambulance man not sure what to do;
mute panic spiralling from him like a twister; the tent poles
of his world collapsing one by one by one.)

i still have the photo of him sitting in the garden inside
the old red phone box mum bought when british telecom
were selling them off cheap. she kept her spades in there,
her trowels, her garden rakes.
mum loved the garden.
grampa loved it too.
we lived on a treeless hill.
the wind tore across it like my father's murderous
breath ripping heads off daisies leaving bewildered
stalks poking from a bloodless lawn.
when nanny died, grampa came to live on the treeless hill.
he didn't do much those months. just stood on the hill
smoking   staring   smoking some more.
mum took him on a cruise; a change of scene; fresh sea air;
a new place to smoke. he had his photo taken with the captain.
when i look at that photo now, it's not grampa's best navy blazer
i see, nor the pink garland around his neck celebrating
the sea princess's arrival into hawaii; but the slow puncture
of his grief leaking soundlessly from his soul.
when he got too frail to stand up to the wind on the hill
he took to sitting inside the phone box among the spades
the trowels, the garden rakes and from his quiet, windless

interior, smoke fag
after fag after
fag.
all too soon he got too frail for the phone box. ended
up in the hospital. my sister rang every night from london
to ask how he was. the night after he died i picked up the receiver
and heard myself tell her he was fine. i have never been one
for delivering bad news. when i placed the phone back
on its cradle i wandered out onto the treeless
hill, carrying the terrible lie, searching
for somewhere to hide it.

who shot jr?

then we got bored of the beheadings on youtube

then the arsehole in north korea

then the two hundred and seventy six schoolgirls taken
in nigeria by boko haram

then the campaign to bring the girls home—#BringBackOurGirls
scribbled onto a piece of cardboard & held up for the cameras—
*(as if a piece of cardboard and a few celebrities was ever going
to bring them all home*)*

then in among all of that aussie blokes are murdering fifty
two women a year

then eleven thousand three hundred and fifteen people
died of ebola and we got bored seeing that on the telly every night too

then the bushfires came

and the news station put a soundtrack to the devastation—footage
of firefighters running towards the flames in slow motion
before cutting to a commercial break
giving us just enough time to grab a giant
popcorn and a litre of diet coke before plonking ourselves
back in front of the telly with the same misplaced eagerness
we felt waiting to find out who shot jr.

now christians and muslims are tiptoeing through the tulips
and around each other and we're all so worried about

offending we're gargling with bleach before
opening our mouths

then i stop at a cafe to buy a coffee and a brownie

the white aussie barista with the hipster beard and too
skinny jeans hears my accent. asks where i'm from

i tell him i'm from scotland. he doesn't reply.
disappears into his milk jug as though commenting
on someone else's nationality was an over-chlorinated
swimming pool he was not prepared to dive into

then my friend working as a waiter in a fancy
restaurant was asked by two of the diners where he was from

my friend asks them to guess

the diners take turns stabbing at various
exotic locations—none of them correct

my friend tells them he's from india

ah! they said, *we thought you were from india, but we didn't
want to say so in case we insulted you*

i try to tease the hipster boy's nose out of his milk
jug—ask him if he's been to scotland before

he says no, but he'd love to go—only not in winter, ha ha ha—
and the ice between us is broken

he asks me how long i've been in australia
i tell him twenty four years

the hipster boy says nothing, pours my coffee, dusts
it in chocolate, squeezes a lid on top and hands it to me along
with my brownie and my three dollars change and says,
okay, well, uhm, enjoy your coffee and uhm, welcome to
australia—i guess?

i take my coffee, my brownie and my three dollar
change and i tiptoe out of cafe that day thinking
#nooneknowswhatthefucktosayanymore

* *Five years later about 100*
of the 276 Nigerian girls are still missing
(TRT World Now, April 2019)

hate is a thing without feathers

i have always hated my thighs. *(is hate too strong a word?)*
if hate were a thing with feathers i could hold my own gaze
in the mirror longer than three seconds. when she first married
him the worst word my mother could think of to say was hate.
she lived with him for forty-three years. with time her vocabulary
grew—significantly. eventually she was up there with the best
of them, pulling one profanity after another from her once feather
lined throat like albino rabbits from a magician's top hat.
when i read Ben Lerner's poem and get to his line, '... *every time,*
he says, breasts are described in the poems of men, a woman
undergoes mastectomy ...' i glance down at my own, diminished
since the starvation. from there my eyes collapse onto the exhausted
plateau of my thighs spreading over the edges of my chair like
pancake batter thrown carelessly into a cold frying pan
by a disinterested chef. in the days before god was born
these thighs were so firm birds could have perched on them,
lost themselves in the fertile plain of stoic vegetation that grew
and grew and asked nothing in return. hair no longer sprouts
from their lukewarm inners now. tumbleweed could blow
through the sagging thigh-gap i used to think was the meaning
of life. *what weighs more – twenty kilos of hate or twenty*
kilos of coal? in the daylight hours i cover my thighs in black,
sometimes blue. i wear my pants loose. i cannot bear to be
contained in close quarters to my own skin. at night i wear
my mother's pyjama bottoms. navy blue with clusters of tiny
pink stars fizzing away like a thousand champagne
bubbles with nothing to celebrate.

the dandruff in the dry scalp of your longing

PART i

slip off the concrete boots of your dreams

scrape what's left of your soul spread too thin between
the bricks of your debt, apply vitamin E cream to the burns
from the noose around your neck—

let   your   dreams   rise

like gnocchi to the surface of your pan. rescue them
with a draining spoon pile them into a bowl pour
on some oil, it will stop them congealing into the solid
mass that nags in the night as your reflux nags when
you forget to take your proton pump inhibitor. stab
your fork into the dream at the top of your pile,
the one that goes,

*if i could pay off my mortgage, i'd … [insert your own dream here—
it will make the poem more real].*

now sit back. make yourself comfortable. take a deep
breath in and focus on my pocket watch swinging slowly
from side to side. i am going to count from one to ten now.
when i get to ten you will know exactly how it feels
to have paid off your mortgage and [*insert your own dream here*].

one. you are breathing deeper and deeper.

two. you are feeling sleepier and sleepier. your eyelids are becoming
heavier and heavier.

three. listen. what do you hear? the sparrows
in the trees? the wind rustling through its branches?

four. or is that the sound of your internal metronome
ticking away the neglected hours in the congealed gnocchi
of your existence?

five. keep breathing.

six. your dream is a solitary tadpole now swimming
furiously upstream in the direction of your ovary of possibility.

seven. you are going deeper still.

eight. your dream of [*insert your own dream here*]
is burrowing under your skin now.

nine. it has found its way into your blood.

and ten. your dream has seeped into the soft marrow
of your bones now. it has slid practically unnoticed into
the dilated cells just beneath the surface of your skin
you are flushed pink with it. and the exhilaration
feels something like the first time he kisses
you and your mind is blown and you feel you could
wash all the bed linen, peel the potatoes, simmer
the stew, plough through the ironing and walk
the dog (*twice*) all in one morning.

and in this euphoric state you find you can even ignore
the piercing sounds of your crying child in her ikea cot,
because somewhere inside you, you know your child
will not die because you dare to dream. but that
you just might if you don't.

PART ii

and in your deep hypnotic state
you will not eat a raw onion nor remove all your clothes
in front of an audience full of strangers, but you will feel
liberated and you will walk taller than before as though
you were the queen of this land in an emerald crusted
crown which is two sizes too small and presses
into your forehead causing your head to swell to the size
of a space hopper.

and in your new debt-freeness
you will attract many new friends who will look up to you,
as well they should, and as you walk (or drive in your new
audi Q6) to the local cafe, your many new friends will line
the pavement to catch a glimpse of you and they will hope
the merest molecule of your magic dust will land upon
their lapels and mingle with the dandruff from the dry
scalps of their longing.

and you will look down upon each of them
up to their unshaved armpits in debt and deep into the
emerald envy in the motes of their eyes and once inside
the cafe you will order a bacon and egg roll with not one
egg but two and you will order it with a self assuredness
you never had when you had seven hundred thousand
dollars worth of debt encased in the concrete boots
of your dreams.

and you will no longer need to rake
in the bottom of your handbag for loose coins tangled
in bits of toilet paper you once blew your nose on, but will
now hand over your debit card to the girl behind the counter
who asks which account and you will say SAVINGS in a voice
both loud and proud and when the transaction goes through
you will smile smugly at the people behind you raking for
coins through their own bits of toilet paper at the bottom
of their bags.

and as you bite into your roll, you will
gaze heavenward in a religious sort of way and you will
thank god under your breath in case anyone in the cafe hears
you because really you are an atheist. but being debt free feels
so surreal that you are starting to wonder if maybe god really
does exist and i am going to count backwards from ten now.
when i get to *one*, you will be back in the lounge room
of your debt-laden life with your crying child and your unpaid
bills spread out on the desk bit of your ikea storage unit
and tomorrow morning you will take your anti-depressant
and you will not wash all the bed linen, peel the potatoes,
simmer the stew, plough through the ironing nor walk
the dog (*even once*) and you will know in the soft marrow
of your bones that god really does not exist and you will slip
the noose of your reality back around your neck as the dying
cinders of your dream of one day [*insert your own dream here*]
sink to the bottom of your pan along with your concrete boots
and the uncooked gnocchi of your dreams.

the cumquats of christmas past

you hailed your taxi tuesday the eighteenth
of february 2014 at four twenty seven pm.
i watched it approach, swerve to the kerb
its back doors fly open—if this was death i saw it
crouched behind the wheel & jaded as a night
shift driver full of red bull & no doz & cheap 7/11
coffee ten thousand cigarette butts spewing
from its ashtray's filthy mouth

the driver bundled you in—no fanfare
no prayers no bach cantata sung sotto voce
that might accompany you on the fresh black
tarmac of your new road ahead—& nothing
soft for you to lay your head on

just a cracked vinyl seat stale cigarette
smoke a strawberry scented christmas tree jiggling
like a tea bag from the rear view mirror. i lay my
hand on yours leaned in whispered something like
i'm sorry made sure your pyjama sleeves were clear
of the door before pressing it closed as the first

    bubbles of fermenting sadness rose in me
and i forced them down like cumquats into a jar
filled with brandy in preparation for christmas
which was still ten months away & for weeks i kept
cramming till the skins of my cumquats tore,
their flesh bled out & you could no longer
tell where one cumquat ended & another
began

    & when finally christmas came i half
decked my halls, whispered infrasonic compliments
of the season too low even for a passing whale, hung
empty stockings from the mantle their gaping mouths
speechless by an un-kindled fire & when finally
lunch was served & those of us left were gathered over
turkey & ham i took my jar of preserved cumquats
from the dark of my pantry, made my way around
the table heaping everyone's plate with a side of my
    compressed orange grief.

if you came tapping at the window

we ate indian takeaway that night you died.
when i walked into the taj mahal to pick up our pre-
ordered chicken vindaloo, bombay potatoes and no doubt
complimentary pakoras, sanjit welcomed me, as he had every other
night on our way home from the hospital when we hadn't
the mind for cooking either. *the lady from australia
is here!* he'd announce excitedly, when i'd walk in through
the door. only tonight he spoke softer, came out from behind
his bejewelled counter, clasped his hand gently over
mine, as if he knew. it was foggy that night you died.
when i went to bed i closed my bedroom curtains in case
you'd appear through the pea soup like something
out of a bad horror movie. then i lay down on my side,
my good ear on the pillow, deaf ear in the air,
so if you did come tapping at the window
with a message from the dead i wouldn't
need to hear it.

an arsenal of lidless tupperware in the parched prairie of your existence

if you want to write a novel, novella
or even a poem what you can do is, you can do a writing
course. they are available on the internet. first you must click
on the link then enter your details then you must pay your
too much money using paypal or visa or american express.

once you have paid your too much
money the course people will email you a receipt then
they will send you a password and the password will come
in a separate email for security purposes. when you start
your writing course the course people will give you some
tips and they will call these tips 'techniques' and sometimes
they will call these techniques 'tools' and you will feel like
you are a carpenter or a builder or even a plumber
and when the course is finished you will not employ any
of the tools and techniques you have learnt because you will find
there are still too many other reasons why you are still not writing
such as cleaning the caked-on grease from around the knobs
of your cooker, hoovering the top of your wardrobe and sorting
out the mountain of lidless tupperware containers that avalanche
to the kitchen linoleum each time you open the pantry door.

if by some miracle you do manage
to start writing your novel, novella or even your poem
you may find, despite the fact you are applying your tools
and techniques, that one day you will wake and you will

not be able to write another fucking word and this will be
called writers' block. if you should find yourself with
writers' block what you can do is, you can google on the
internet again and you will find there is a course which
will cure you completely and there will be many courses
to choose from but you will settle on the one called
The Twelve Step Cure for Writer's Block which
makes it sound like alcoholic's anonymous, only
you do not have to be an alcoholic to do this course,
though some of the course participants may be.

when you are not googling courses
on how to write your novel, novella or even your poem
you may also attend too many sessions at writers' festivals.
and one day you will hear paul muldoon speaking at the sydney
writers' festival and he will tell a room crammed full of people
with colour-coded tupperware systems that writing
a poem is like you are building something or constructing
something, and because the room you are in is staring
out at the sydney harbour bridge he will tell you that each
side of the bridge was built at the same time and when
the two sides met in the middle there was a two-centimetre
gap. and he will say it's in the two-centimetre gap where
the poem lives.

and paul will say many other
things too, with his lilt that soothes like someone
is rowing you on a boat on a warmish afternoon after
a picnic of ham sandwiches and a bottle of american
cream soda on the banks of lough mourne.

and in the q&a bit at the end a man
in the audience will stand and he will wait for a microphone
to come and when it comes he will try to be very fancy by
starting with a quote from yeats, then he will ask his question.
and he will be trying so hard to be fancy that no one
will understand what the fuck he is trying to say including
paul muldoon and the man will sit down with the shame
that fills the room like a cheese-plant in a greenhouse
in far north queensland.

and then there will be another
man in the audience and he will ask about how to write
a poem and paul will say many things. and the man will
write the many things down and the tupperware people
will write the many things down too. and paul will say every
poem he writes is an adventure, that he never knows where
it might end up and that sometimes when he reads
back his work it almost feels like he's had no hand in its making.
and he will say all of this looking out from the stage across
a sea of hairy crowns and he will say unto the hairy crowns
that when you are writing a poem, it is important to know—
but it is crucial to not know. and the hairy crowns
will write this thing down too.

and paul will say everything
with his voice that sounds like caramel, if caramel could
be a sound, and quavers and minims and semi-crotchets
will tinkle from his lips like they were tinkling from cathleens'
falls in county donegal and for forty-five minutes the people
will forget about their greasy knobs and the tops of their
wardrobes and their arsenals of lidless tupperware.

and when the session is over
the people will feel unstoppable and they will step out
into the sydney sun and they will see many people from
the writers' festival jotting in their moleskine notebooks
with the soft thick pages that cost thirty-seven dollars
a piece and you too will step out into the sydney sun
and order your cup of tea in a cafe and remove your own
brand new moleskine notebook from its packet, carefully
concealing the $2 writing pads you normally buy
at the supermarket. and you will survey the people
filling their moleskines with their dreams and you will
know somewhere inside you, somewhere small a mouse
might live, that it's possible to write a poem on just about
anything including your greasy knobs, the top of your
wardrobe, even your arsenal of lidless tupperware.

and when you get home
you will put in a load of washing and fry up the mushrooms
and boil the brussel sprouts and you will prepare the cheese
and pickle sandwiches for the following day's lunches
only you will tear your fucking hair out trying to find
lids for your tupperware containers.

many days will pass.
your note taking will dwindle till the moleskine notebook
filled with your dreams disappears down behind the couch
of your longing along with the embryo of your novel, novella
and even your poems and you will find yourself back in the
parched prairie of your existence, with the tumbleweed and
the ennio morricone soundtrack whistling through the canal

of your inner ear. and the poems whose breath you swear
you could feel on the back of your neck will give way
to the knobs and the wardrobe and the tupperware
again.

then one morning, early,
like say five o'clock, you will open the eyes
that dared not dream, your nose will twitch and the sure
smell of your novel, novella and all of your poems
will be gone. and all you will be left with is the ghostly
whiff of hospital potatoes and low-sodium chicken and other
dying odours that linger in antiseptic corridors long after
the dinner trolley is gone and the dead have been moved
to the morgue. and after many months you will be back
on the internet looking at courses again clicking on links
and forgetting the password to your fucking paypal account
and you will know in the small place that you are searching
for a course that will turn you into a writer, without
actually having to write.

and one morning,
early, like say *four* o'clock, you will open the eyes
that suddenly dare to dream and you will know
in the small place if you want to write what you must
do is pick up your pen and press the nib against
the paper in the writing pad which is not soft
and thick and does not cost thirty-seven dollars.
and you will have to do this for many hours and days
and the earth will orbit the sun many times and eventually
things will appear on the two-dollar page you never

thought possible. and each time you sit down to write
you will feel more and more like indiana jones
and sometimes when you read back what you've
written you will be amazed you could write something
so good and it will feel like you had no hand in its making
—and other times you will read back what you've written
and you will be equally amazed—but it will be for very
different reasons.

if you have no eyes where do the tears go?

the emotions are half price on tuesdays.
you are lured in after your father's funeral
by the fluoro lights bright as the mushroom
cloud you're not meant to look directly into
lest it burn the eyes right out of your fucking
head—

if you have no eyes, where do the tears go?

you go inside. pull your collar up, sink your
unexpectedly wet face into the V of your jumper.
make like the woman who cut the coupon from
the newspaper & won the three-minute trolley
dash at the local supermarket.

take a trolley that does not require the coin
you never have:

> *on your mark.*

> *get set.*

> *go.*

aisle 1
baked beans, corned beef, two fruits in syrup, sadness.
move quickly. sadness is on special. take a dozen cans.
check date. make sure it has long best before.

aisle 2
ajax, napisan, stain remover, disappointment.
throw in a dozen cans of disappointment.
reconsider. take spares.

aisle 3
toothpaste, mouth wash, sanitary towels, anger.
empty shelves of anger. get second trolley. advise
girl on tannoy you will need assistance to the car.

aisle 4
dog meat, cat litter, sardines, regret. throw in a few,
but then again too few to mention.

[*turn out of aisle four, past the yoghurts culturing
better days, the free range eggs in their supermarket
cage, the low fat cottage cheese you used to buy
in your teens when you were trying to disappear*]

aisle 5
frozen peas, dim sim, linda mccartney hot dogs,
forgiveness—seeping from freezers like fog.
wipe a circle in the condensation on the glass
door, press your eye up against it, stare in at the
piles of forgiveness stacked neatly in convenient
250 g blocks. open the door. take a single block
in your hand. it is lighter than you imagined. turn
to your trolley already overflowing with the anger
& the rage, the disappointment & the hardly any
regret & consign the 250 g block of forgiveness
back to its fog.

aisle 6

strawberry ice cream, coconut fro-yo, lemon
sorbet, comfort. take ten tubs of comfort, two
of the sorbet, four of the coconut fro-yo—though
you do not really know what fro-yo is, it sounds
like it might be happiness.

make way to check out. pile half-price emotions
on conveyor belt. pay your bill. the girl tannoys
for car assistance. once in your car you momentarily
consider going back for even just one single block
of forgiveness. you decide against it. turn the key
in your ignition. head for the exit.
forgiveness is on ice. you
know it will keep.

once upon a time in shanghai

i

was

a

balloon

once––

so full of helium i had to be scraped off the ceiling.
back then i could come home from work, paint the lounge walls
green, make a curry, vacuum the carpet, walk the dog, write a book.
back then it was like i was powered by solar panels in the blistering
bush. back then it was like i was a cannula in the vein of a sun that would
never clot & die. look at the thin membrane of my balloon now—look at my
stretched flappy arm skin crinkled like a length of loose glad wrap sagging on
a bowl of fresh custard. how many more days are there? i swallow down my
days like i'm dutifully finishing up a packet of expired gluten-free shortbreads
bought in error & couldn't be returned. in the poem the chinese man returns
to shanghai to die. i sandwich the weight of the poem between my depressed
husband's palms. his eyes nibble at the crusts of its lines, arms slip into the
jacket of its filling. imagine, i tell him no more crumbs in the unmade
beds of our days / the rings of our jupiters no longer hula hooping in
our congealed milky ways / the final flutter of our white flags grey
from waving in surrender / imagine that soft warm earth
in our ears / the petering flames of our suns going
down / imagine,

i urge him /

the stars

no longer

in our

eyes.

who's a pretty boy then?

how is your soul? your unleashed fears that too
quickly filled the corners of your mind before
the too fast river of them burst into alcoves
and crannies you didn't even know you had and budgie
mirrors on chains swung violently from side to side with the chaos
of your terror spraying bird seed from here to hell
as your worn-out beak tapped out an SOS on the cuttle-
fish of your confusion and the tiny bells tied
to your cage tolled as your justified despair
magnified through the +10 lenses of your tears
spilled over and filled the room like an oversized
elephant saying who's a pretty fucking
boy then?

not much of a mother in four parts:
part IV

i'd have buried her by the scots pines in the cemetery
lush and green, strewn with clover and buttercups yellow
as the yolks of the fried eggs we'd have for breakfast
on sunday mornings. and where are the four-leafed
clovers now that i need them? we used to make daisy
chains here together, just the two of us in our matching
pink sun hats with the corks that hung from the brim my sister
sent us all the way from australia. and my how we'd laugh
as the bobbing corks chased away midges that dared come
too close. and the soft pink cotton shaded our heads
from the fading embers of the afternoon sun as it slid down
and fell off the end of my world. and i know she's too little
to know the beauty of this place right now but when she's older
i know that she will. and she'll know i chose this spot in the shade
of the pines with their roots digging deep into the earth reaching
for their own molten cores to drink the love they'll need
to stand another hundred years protecting my daughter
from the warm rays of the summers to come and freezing
winds that will whistle in bleak winter days here and dark
lonely nights. and the snow queen will cover this place
with her blanket of snow and ghosts of dead children
will make their Olafs with gouged-out holes for eyes,
a carrot for a nose and lumps of coal for buttons
down the front of their iced winter coats
that no one can see.

mr sausage

i had other names for him besides hector.
a woman on the beach heard me call him bubbles once.
then mr sausage. she stopped to pat him, *so his name's*
bubbles? she asked. *no* i said. awkwardly. *it's hector.*
then she asked about the mr sausage thing only i didn't
have an answer except he loves sausages. by that rationale
i could also have called him mr bacon, mr pizza, mr sticky
date pudding, mr ben & jerry's new york fudge, mr t-bone
steak, señor paella, herr chicken schnitzel, monsieur ratatouille.
the only names i could never have called him were mr tahini,
mr alfalfa sprout, mr cucumber crudite.
i suspect dog owners who say,
oh you should get another dog have yet to find themselves
soaking in the too much garlic marinade of loss that seeps deep
into the folds of the chicken tenderloins of their existence.
then they bang on about how the joy a dog brings far outweighs
the sadness once they're gone. *does it?* i say, pulling
my jumper out at the neck and staring down towards
my heart that still houses the grief i thought would only
be on a short-term lease but is still there, with its three-
piece suite, its king-size bed, its louis the XV dining
table with eight matching chairs.
it's been three years.
my heart is still fragile. getting another dog now
would be like biting into a chocolate liqueur. the structure
of the chocolate case cannot withstand the pressure of my bite.

the entire thing collapses. sticky liqueur squirts from my mouth
dribbles down onto the collar of my white silk shirt.
i take the shirt to the dry cleaner. he has seen these stains before.

he points to his arsenal of stain-removing chemicals—one for
sausages, one for pizza, one for unrelenting grief.

he tells me he will do his best
but he cannot promise
anything.

when your father dies of nothing

you turn yourself inside-out like eyelids.
you look and you look and you don't stop looking
and you're on your knees shining the torch under
the walnut buffet of your youth where you usually

find the answer to everything but still you come up
with nothing. then you find yourself down the back
of the couch with the loose coins and the stale crisps
and the piece of lego that left your castle without

a turret and your distressed damsel with nowhere
to hide. then you find yourself rummaging through
the kitchen drawer where you keep the plans for the
extension you never built and the card from the vet
saying how sorry he was about the dog. then the other
card about the cat.

and you look and you look and you don't stop looking
and sometimes you hover like a tiny drone in the sip of air
between the shower screen and the bathroom cabinet where
mildew spreads like cancer. then you're back in a country

that isn't scotland and you're ankle deep in rock pools
with the crabs and the sea dragons and the bits of seaweed
and the other crabs (the small ones you can't eat) but still
you don't see the thing you're looking for.

and sometimes when the sun goes down, weirdly you
turn to god (and sometimes the universe, which is another
sort of god) but you don't find it there either. then you ask
your friend with the crystals who does the hot yoga then

the woman in the next street who did the reiki on the dog
before he died then the old greek woman who knows
everything and speaks with the dead.

then you google chaos theory and minor perturbations
caused by butterfly wings and you limp every day another
bit closer to the day when none of it matters anymore, but
still you keep looking as though the world were somehow
meant be pink and cloudless, comprehensible and fair.

i didn't think i would die like this

too many years out here with no one
except the fawny kangaroos that come
by, their joeys poking out their pouches
looking for food, the cheek of them
when the orange sun that's roared all
day starts to fade and the pink dusk
rolls in and brings a coolness
money couldn't buy you.

> i sit here on my veranda
> from dawn to dusk

watch the early morning sun rise up
from the other side of the world quivering
in the heat waves that tell me it's going
to be another scorcher—this is australia
after all. mid-morning sun's the worst.
unforgiving rays barge through my lace
iron fence branding the backs of my hands
and arms leaving me brown and patterned
like a hennaed indian bride.

we laughed when we first saw this place
a settler's cottage with its very own
flagpole standing to attention in the neglected
front yard—its once white paint now grey
and flaking with a tattered australian flag
fluttering half heartedly, half mast.

we took the flag down when we moved
in—always said we'd grow honeysuckle
up the pole but we never did

> just like we talked about
> heading back to scotland
> and france to what little roots
> we had but we never
> did that either.

we spent our days on this deck—him chain
smoking himself to death, me drinking
myself the same way and i can tell you every
groove and every knot in every plank. he used
to creosote them trying to preserve
them from the searing heat. he was already
blind by then but it didn't stop him feeling
his way the length of the wood with his brush
loaded up with too much creosote, christ,
he was useless at it. i can still see
the planks he missed and the rage
i felt at him having missed them

> the outrage of the untreated
> planks that had felt so justified

back then and my planks are worse
neglected now, they've dried out completely
and how could they not? sure i haven't the mind
for preserving them now. not at this time in my life

when all i've left in me is the energy to get
from my bed to my beloved deck. and i know
it's daft but i can still feel him here beside
me rocking away in that bloody chair
of his that squeaked and groaned every
time he tipped it forwards to flick his fag
ash into the still neglected
front yard.

> we left sydney fourteen
> years ago, groaned in unison
> as we drove past

the massive billboard on victoria road
with the commonwealth bank ad
showcasing the grey-haired couple towing
a caravan, happy and fucking smiling
with the caption commanding us all to
really start living now that we've retired.
and people asked us, but what are you going to *do*
in your retirement? as if it were for doing
things in. they just stared blankly
when we announced we had no plans to

> travel round australia
> climb mount everest

jump out of a fucking plane take a tour
of the great sandy desert on a harley
davidson with a side car.

people fear death

they fill their lives with stuff
as if staying busy might somehow
allow them to outrun it. i stopped
fearing death a long time ago.
i myself am ready for it now

        my arms are open
        wide i will welcome
        it like a long lost
        child.

this dilapidated cottage was all
we could afford. sydney had bled
us dry, we had no choice but to move
out here to the middle of fucking
nowhere—a township they call it—
a few shitty houses, a pub, the lucky
harbour chinese, a milk bar that
doubles as a post office where
you can pay your bills send
a fax or buy a stamp

        if you're still in the mood
        for staying in touch

no internet to speak of, though there's talk
of them cabling soon, but we don't hold
our breaths. until then our lives remain
facebookless, twitterless, instagram free.

and there's a supermarket—i use the term
loosely—from another time, maybe even the time
of the first settlers judging by the thickness
of the dust on the cornflakes, the canned
dog food that sits incongruously alongside
the tampons, the basket of marked down
out-of-date pine nuts and star anise
that tell the story of shopkeepers alone
in their desire for change.

> thomas found it easier
> to settle here than me,
> well his heart is kinder
> than mine—listen

to me, talking about him as if he's still here.
it's been four years already. and i think of him every
day especially when the breeze that comes
in the night blows his rocking chair forward
and the bloody thing creaks and groans
as if he were still in it. people tell me
i'll get over the sadness, that time's
a great healer, that life goes fucking on
but i don't want my memories of him
to fade, to forget the shape of his nose
the long black curl of his lashes, the shadow
of his akubra across his brow as he rocked
himself to sleep on that bloody rocking
chair of his.

i miss everything about
him. jesus christ, i even
miss the smell of his gitanes.

and we did our best
to be good australians

we really did. ate the char siu beef
and the chicken in black bean sauce
once a week at the lucky harbour chinese.
christ, we even drank the house red
in there and believe me that wasn't
easy. and as we ate i'd have to avert
my gaze from the tropical fish tank
in the window. five motionless fish mourning
the loss of family and friends. a crumpled
poster of the ocean stuck to the back
of the tank attempting to fool the fish
they're still in their turquoise sea.

people ask

if i'd go back now and live out my final days
in scotland or france but i tell them no. i won't
go now and leave my thomas buried alone
here in this red parched land.

so i'll die here in australia too.
what's good enough for my thomas
is good enough for me.

all the offal love

when it all draws to a close—
will
i
have
iced
my
cake
thickly?
will i have left the imprint of my fingertips
in the soft yellow marzipan of my days? when
the tungsten coil of the twenty-watt bulb i always
said i'd replace with something brighter, *pfoofs*
& dies with all the certainty of an 18 to 35-year-old
male suicide in the bush, will my performance
on the parallel bars of my life be judged by good god,
with marks out of ten on holy score
cards in the sky?
or
a
nastier
one
who rejoices in rubbing my nose in the pishy
carpet of my failings? when i get to the end of my
days will i have stretched my stomach thin & transparent,
wrapped it around the haggis of my heart, stuffed
it with all the offal love & tender hate (*which*

is really just another sort of love)?
will i
acknowledge
the
hate
grew
of
its
own
accord—
that despite my burying it deep in the crocus
bowl of my winters, sliding it under the dark side of
my bed, pulling the door shut tight, still its thin green arms
grew, stretched out across the carpet reaching for its mother,
demanding to be fed. what sort of a mother can ignore
her bawling child? i should have let it die. instead
i fed it till it was fat with formula & heavy
with blooms so terrifying a pink even
the
bees
wouldn't
go
near.
sometimes when i'm driving back from the supermarket
i consider the possibility i may not make it home alive.
when i pull into my driveway & i'm not dead, i unpack
the car, marvel at the canned spaghetti & sliced white bread

i'll get to enjoy if i make it into the house without breaking
my neck on the stairs & every other day i don't die, i try
to go to bed eager. wake up glad. i do my best to whip
the egg whites of my love till they stand in peaks
of their own accord. i sift my light like flour.
churn my hate till it turns to butter.

postscript

this is coal don't be afraid

if you are in or close to the bush leave now. if you choose to stay we may not be able to save you. save any woollen blankets you may have wrap yourself in them when the fire comes there is no better place to raise kids. if you are trapped in your car face towards the oncoming fire tightly close windows and doors get down below window level this is your highest priority. the prime minister regrets any offence caused to anyone for him being away at this time of crisis. for those of you in fire affected [insert town name here] it is now too late to leave. the girls and jen will stay on and stay out the rest of the time we had booked here, we will not be changing our climate policy settings. but i'm comforted by the fact that australians would like me to be here, just simply so i can be here, alongside them as they're going through this terrible time how good is hawaii? if you don't have a Bush Fire Smoke Respirator P2 Aura Flat Fold mask including valve 9322A+ (max 2 packets per customer, was $94.95 now $77.45) stay indoors. i don't hold a hose mate but i understand people are angry people are hurting. this is coal don't be scared don't be afraid seek shelter from the heat of the fire. but look, the girls and jen, they love holidaying in hawaii and so we've had a few nice days here. drink water to prevent dehydration evacuate your horse to the beach have your children row for their lives. australians will be inspired by the great feats of our cricketers this is not about climate change we are meeting and beating our paris agreement targets how good's australia? to the five hundred million species we burned how good's the cricket? you won't be getting any votes down here buddy you're an idiot leave the pregnant woman's hand alone. the sky will turn black turn your headlights on. you're out son. do you have a bush fire survival plan? activate it.

This is a found poem made up of statements by Scott Morrison, our Prime Minister, by our Rural Fire Service and residents of fire-affected communities, and a tweet from someone offering advice on what to do if you are in the path of an oncoming fire.

My heart goes out to all those affected by these fires, to all the animals, birds, reptiles and insects we have decimated. To our firefighters, my eternal admiration and gratitude. And my deepest apologies go out to the land we treat in the way that we do.

acknowledgements

Some of these poems were first published in the following magazines, anthologies and journals:

The Moth, American Journal of Poetry, Pittsburgh Quarterly Review, Tahoma Literary Review, Canberra Times, Honest Ulsterman, Poethead, Glasgow Review of Books, Bareknuckle Poet, Bangor Literary Journal, Poets' Republic, Burning House Press, Live Encounters, Dodging The Rain, The Blue Nib, Headstuff, Galway Review, Squawk Back, Ink, Sweat & Tears, Husk, Forty Voices Strong: an Anthology of Contemporary Scottish Poetry, Cordite Poetry Review & The Hunter Writers Centre Grief Anthology.

I am deeply indebted to everyone at Wakefield Press and in particular editor extraordinaire Julia Beaven and director Michael Bollen, and to anyone who's ever commented on a poem, liked or shared a post, bought a book or responded so generously to my work, including Alexandra Neville, Karen O'Brien, Kri Ackers, Magi Gibson, Ian Macpherson, Bron Coleman, Anne Casey, Izzy Whitelock, Andrew Whitelock, Fiona McCormick & Mum.

Wakefield Press is an independent publishing and
distribution company based in Adelaide, South Australia.
We love good stories and publish beautiful books.
To see our full range of books, please visit our website at
www.wakefieldpress.com.au
where all titles are available for purchase.
To keep up with our latest releases, news and events,
subscribe to our monthly newsletter.

Find us!

Facebook: www.facebook.com/wakefield.press
Twitter: www.twitter.com/wakefieldpress
Instagram: www.instagram.com/wakefieldpress